FUTURES & OPTIONS
CONTRACTS SPECIFICATIONS

John Wilmore – Athens 2016

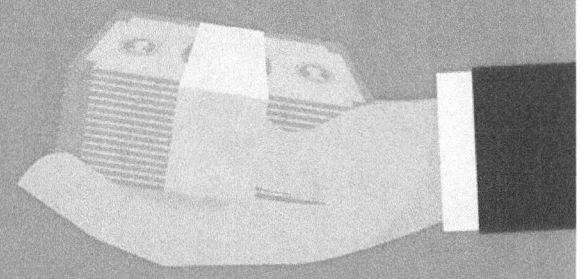

John Wilmore - Athens 2016

DEDICATION

To my beautiful wife and kids

PREFACE

Unlike stocks, derivatives are shunned by most retail investors. Why is that? There are four reasons I can think of. First there is the complex mathematics that put some people off, second there is the leverage that is too tempting to abuse, third is the negative publicity associated with some over-the-counter derivatives, and lastly the jargon that is often used by traders. Terms such as "in the money", "out of the money", "tick size", "exercise", "front month" and "back month" to name a few can be quite intimidating.

Yet, those who overcome their fears and understand the risks get rewarded with a global market understanding that touches almost every aspect of economic activity. There is no better way to get an idea of where the market thinks the world is heading than to be able to follow the derivatives markets.

There are many books that cover the theory behind derivatives. Some books even give specifics on trading techniques for a specific asset class, such as commodities or bonds. I own and like a lot of them. However, what I thought was lacking was a handbook that focused on the actual instruments used out there, in the real world. The instruments: with which hedge funds make their money; with which banks and industrials hedge their exposure; and on which speculators bet their dollars.

With this handbook, I try to keep things simple. I assume you've just gotten your feet wet and have deciphered at least part of the jargon, but you still need some practical tools to put things in perspective. So what I've done is singled out 89 instruments from 11 categories and picked out the features that I believe represent the basic building blocks you need to use these yourselves. In this way, you'll have enough introductory material to follow the financial news on TV before you get down to trading.

The selection methodology is based entirely on my personal trading preference and exposure as a trader. You may choose to adopt your own preferences once you gain experience.

Go Ahead. Take the Plunge. You'll be rewarded.

John Wilmore.

Athens, 2016.

TABLE OF CONTENTS

PREFACE.......................... 9

INTRODUCTION 15

CATEGORY 1 - AGRICULTURE.......... 17

CATEGORY 2 - BONDS 25

CATEGORY 3 - CURRENCIES............ 40

CATEGORY 4 - EMISSIONS 55

CATEGORY 5 - ENERGY.................... 57

CATEGORY 6 - EQUITY INDICES...... 63

CATEGORY 7 - VOLATILITY 95

CATEGORY 8 - INTEREST RATES..... 97

CATEGORY 9 - LIVESTOCK............. 103

CATEGORY 10 - METALS................ 107

CATEGORY 11 – SOFTS................... 115

INDEX 121

INTRODUCTION

"What is a Eurodollar Future and how is it quoted? When do Gold Options trade and in which Exchange? What is one thing you should know about the VIX Volatility Index?

This book introduces readers to eighty-nine of the world's most popular derivatives markets. Handpicked from thousands of derivative products out there, these 89 products are widely used by retail and institutional investors around the world to hedge their exposure or speculate on equity indices, bonds, currencies and commodities. Written for traders, investors, advisors, brokers, students, and people eager to learn more about exchange traded derivatives, this book gives readers:

- A practical understanding of the underlying instruments

- Contract Specifications and trading hours of electronically traded Futures and Options

- Trading tips and suggestions

- Soft metrics of liquidity, leverage and volatility of each Futures product.

Enjoy!

Category 1 - Agriculture

AGRICULTURE

Corn

United States of America

Used in food products such as flakes, syrup, and sweeteners, and in animal feeds. Roughly 60% of corn ends up as animal feed and 12% on ethanol. Production for bio-ethanol has increased over the last 40 years. US, China, Brazil and Mexico are the main producers.

FUTURES

Symbol	ZC
Electronic Venue	CME-CBT
Exchange Name	Chicago Board of Trade
Contract Size	5,000.00 Bushels
Tick Size	1/4 of one cent
Tick Value	USD 12.5
Quoted in	cents/bushel

OPTIONS

Contract Size	One futures contract
Tick Size	1/8 of one cent
Tick Value	USD 6.25

Day Session | Monday – Friday: 8:30 a.m. – 1:20 p.m.
Night Session | Sunday – Thursday: 7:00 p.m. – 7:45 a.m.
Central Standard Time - Chicago

TRADING TIPS

Weather and seasonality play an important role in the pricing of this commodity. Harvest in the US takes place between September and December. Physical delivery.

LIQUIDITY	**LEVERAGE**	**VOLATILITY**
Low	Low	High

AGRICULTURE

Soybean
United States of America

A major oil seed crop and the second-most valuable agricultural export in the US behind corn (2014). It costs half as much as corn to grow and is preferred by farmers in times of price uncertainty.

FUTURES

Symbol	ZS
Electronic Venue	CME-CBT
Exchange Name	Chicago Board of Trade
Contract Size	5,000.00 Bushels
Tick Size	1/4 of one cent
Tick Value	USD 12.5
Quoted in	cents/bushel

OPTIONS

Contract Size	One futures contract
Tick Size	1/8 of one cent
Tick Value	USD 6.25

Day Session | Monday – Friday: 8:30 a.m. – 1:20 p.m.
Night Session | Sunday – Thursday: 7:00 p.m. – 7:45 a.m.
Central Standard Time - Chicago

TRADING TIPS

The crush spread — the difference between soybean and soybean oil and soybean meal — is actively traded by speculators, processors and hedgers. Physical delivery.

LIQUIDITY   LEVERAGE   VOLATILITY
Medium   Medium   Medium

AGRICULTURE

Wheat

United States of America

Wheat production is second only to corn as an agricultural commodity and is widely grown around the world. China, EU, India, US and Russia are major producers. Prices subject to disruptions, including weather, national controls and competing crops.

FUTURES

Symbol	ZW
Electronic Venue	CME-CBT
Exchange Name	Chicago Board of Trade
Contract Size	5,000.00 Bushels
Tick Size	1/4 of one cent
Tick Value	USD 12.5
Quoted in	cents/bushel

OPTIONS

Contract Size	One futures contract
Tick Size	1/8 of one cent
Tick Value	USD 6.25

Day Session | Monday – Friday: 8:30 a.m. – 1:20 p.m.
Night Session | Sunday – Thursday: 7:00 p.m. – 7:45 a.m.
Central Standard Time - Chicago

TRADING TIPS

The USDA and the CFTC reports are important tools for every grain trader. So are insights on government regulations, subsidies and consumer trends. Physical delivery.

LIQUIDITY	**LEVERAGE**	**VOLATILITY**
Medium	Low	High

AGRICULTURE

Bean Oil
United States of America

A major vegetable oil extracted from soybean seeds. Mainly used in food production but also important in the production of bio-diesel. China, US, Brazil and Argentina the major producers.

FUTURES

Symbol	ZL
Electronic Venue	CME-CBT
Exchange Name	Chicago Board of Trade
Contract Size	60,000.00 lbs
Tick Size	0.0001
Tick Value	USD 6
Quoted in	Cents/lb.

OPTIONS

Contract Size	One futures contract
Tick Size	0.00005
Tick Value	USD 3

Day Session | Monday – Friday: 8:30 a.m. – 1:20 p.m.
Night Session | Sunday – Thursday: 7:00 p.m. – 7:45 a.m.
Central Standard Time - Chicago

TRADING TIPS

Bean Oil constitutes approximately 20% of global edible oil trade volume. It has been in a long downward trend since 2011. Physical delivery.

LIQUIDITY	**LEVERAGE**	**VOLATILITY**
Medium	Medium	High

AGRICULTURE

Soybean Meal
United States of America

Used worldwide as a protein supplement in animal feeds. It is the residue produced during soybean oil extraction.

FUTURES

Symbol	ZM
Electronic Venue	CME-CBT
Exchange Name	Chicago Board of Trade
Contract Size	100.00 Short Tons
Tick Size	0.1
Tick Value	USD 10
Quoted in	USD/short ton

OPTIONS

Contract Size	One futures contract
Tick Size	0.05
Tick Value	USD 5

Day Session | Monday – Friday: 8:30 a.m. – 1:20 p.m.
Night Session | Sunday – Thursday: 7:00 p.m. – 7:45 a.m.
Central Standard Time - Chicago

TRADING TIPS

Watch out for India's monsoon reports as they can have a significant impact on production expectations. Similar fundamentals with soybean and soybean oil apply here. Physical delivery.

LIQUIDITY   LEVERAGE   VOLATILITY

Low   Low   High

AGRICULTURE

Oat

United States of America

A widely grown cereal grain that is commonly used in breakfast food and livestock feed. EU, Russia, Canada, Australia and the US are among the top producers of oat in the world.

FUTURES

Symbol	ZO
Electronic Venue	CME-CBT
Exchange Name	Chicago Board of Trade
Contract Size	5,000.00 Bushels
Tick Size	1/4 of one cent or 0.0025
Tick Value	USD 12.5
Quoted in	USD/bushel

OPTIONS

Contract Size	One futures contract
Tick Size	1/8 of one cent or 0.00125
Tick Value	USD 6.25

Day Session | Monday – Friday: 8:30 a.m. – 1:20 p.m.
Night Session | Sunday – Thursday: 7:00 p.m. – 7:45 a.m.
Central Standard Time - Chicago

TRADING TIPS

Demand for oats can be significantly affected by fluctuations of demand for horse and cattle feed. Physical delivery.

LIQUIDITY	**LEVERAGE**	**VOLATILITY**
Low	Low	High

AGRICULTURE

Rough Rice
United States of America

The most important grain crop is considered a "wage" commodity for workers and is subject to government controls. Production has increased over 40 years; however, population growth and declining yield growth are significant supply constraints going forward.

FUTURES

Symbol	ZR
Electronic Venue	CME-CBT
Exchange Name	Chicago Board of Trade
Contract Size	2,000.00 Cwt (centum weight)
Tick Size	1/2 cent or 0.005
Tick Value	USD 10
Quoted in	USD/cwt

OPTIONS

Contract Size	One futures contract
Tick Size	1/4 cent or 0.0025
Tick Value	USD 5

Day Session | Monday – Friday: 8:30 a.m. – 1:20 p.m.
Night Session | Sunday – Thursday: 7:00 p.m. – 7:45 a.m.
Central Standard Time - Chicago

TRADING TIPS

Increased consumption of rice in China reduces supply available for exports. Global exports are dominated by small producing countries. Physical delivery.

LIQUIDITY	**LEVERAGE**	**VOLATILITY**
Low	Medium	High

Category 2 - Bonds

BOND

Euro-BTP

Italy

Euro-BTP Italian Government Bonds: notional debt instrument issued by the Republic of Italy with a term of 8.5 to 11 years. Original maturity no longer than 16 years. New Futures contracts introduced in Sep. 2011.

FUTURES

Symbol	FBTP
Electronic Venue	EUREX
Exchange Name	Eurex
Contract Size	EUR 100,000.00
Tick Size	0.01
Tick Value	EUR 10
Quoted in	Percentage of par value

Day Session | Monday to Friday: 8:00 a.m. – 7:00 p.m. Central European Time - Frankfurt

TRADING TIPS

A reliable indicator of bond appetite in the European periphery. Volume and open interest have increased substantially since launch. Physical delivery.

LIQUIDITY	**LEVERAGE**	**VOLATILITY**
High	High	Low

BOND
Euro-Bund
Germany

Notional long-term debt instrument issued by the Federal Republic of Germany, with a remaining term of 8.5 to 10.5 years and a coupon of 6%. Bunds at year end 2012 accounted for 60% of the Federal Government's debt portfolio.

FUTURES

Symbol	FGBL
Electronic Venue	EUREX
Exchange Name	Eurex
Contract Size	EUR 100,000.00
Tick Size	0.01
Tick Value	EUR 10
Quoted in	Percentage of par value

Day Session | Monday to Friday: 8:00 a.m. − 10:00 p.m. Central European Time - Frankfurt

OPTIONS

Contract Size	One futures contract
Tick Size	0.01
Tick Value	EUR 10

Day Session | Monday to Friday: 8:00 a.m. − 5:15 p.m. Central European Time - Frankfurt

TRADING TIPS

The indisputable leader of the European bond universe. Highly suitable for hedging or speculating on core European macro themes. Physical delivery.

LIQUIDITY   LEVERAGE   VOLATILITY
High   High   Low

BOND

Euro-Bobl

Germany

Notional Medium-term debt instrument issued by the Federal Republic of Germany, with a remaining term of 4.5 to 5.5 years.

FUTURES

Symbol	FGBM
Electronic Venue	EUREX
Exchange Name	Eurex
Contract Size	EUR 100,000.00
Tick Size	0.01
Tick Value	EUR 10
Quoted in	Percentage of par value

Day Session | Monday to Friday: 8:00 a.m. – 10:00 p.m. Central European Time - Frankfurt

OPTIONS

Contract Size	One futures contract
Tick Size	0.005
Tick Value	EUR 5

Day Session | Monday to Friday: 8:00 a.m. – 5:15 p.m. Central European Time - Frankfurt

TRADING TIPS

A medium term instrument with a lower duration than the Bund. Not as popular with retail traders as the Bund. Physical delivery.

LIQUIDITY	**LEVERAGE**	**VOLATILITY**
High	High	Low

BOND

Euro-Schatz
Germany

A notional short-term debt instrument issued by the Federal Republic of Germany with a term of 1.75 to 2.25 and a coupon of 6%. Federal Treasury Notes (Schaetze) accounted for 12% of the Government's debt portfolio in 2012.

FUTURES

Symbol	FGBS
Electronic Venue	EUREX
Exchange Name	Eurex
Contract Size	EUR 100,000.00
Tick Size	0.005
Tick Value	EUR 5
Quoted in	Percentage of par value

Day Session | Monday to Friday: 8:00 a.m. – 10:00 p.m. Central European Time - Frankfurt

OPTIONS

Contract Size	One futures contract
Tick Size	0.005
Tick Value	EUR 5

Day Session | Monday to Friday: 8:00 a.m. – 5:15 p.m. Central European Time - Frankfurt

TRADING TIPS

A short term instrument, which moves in a tight price range; until ECB rates start moving, in which case fireworks ensue. Physical delivery.

LIQUIDITY	**LEVERAGE**	**VOLATILITY**
High	High	Low

Bond

U.S. Treasury Bond

United States of America

This 30-year Treasury Bond is known as the Long-Bond and it has a $100,000 face value available at auction in $100 increments. You receive interest 6% monthly and the face value on maturity.

FUTURES

Symbol	ZB
Electronic Venue	CME-CBT
Exchange Name	Chicago Board of Trade
Contract Size	USD 100,000.00
Tick Size	1/32 or 0.03125
Tick Value	USD 31.25
Quoted in	points

OPTIONS

Contract Size	One futures contract
Tick Size	1/64 or 0.015625
Tick Value	USD 15.625

Continuous | Sunday – Friday: 5:00 p.m. – 4:00 p.m. with a one hour break from 4:00 p.m. to 5:00 p.m. every day except Friday, which closes at 4:00 p.m.
Central Standard Time - Chicago

TRADING TIPS

The 30-year Treasury Bond used to be the bellwether US bond. It was reintroduced in 2006 after a four year suspension. An investment preferred by most pension funds. Physical delivery.

LIQUIDITY	**LEVERAGE**	**VOLATILITY**
High	High	Medium

BOND

10-Year T-Note
United States of America

10-year Treasury Notes have a $100,000 face value. You receive interest 6% monthly and the face value on maturity. Now all electronic, they can be sold and bought at auction in $100 denominations.

FUTURES

Symbol	ZN
Electronic Venue	CME-CBT
Exchange Name	Chicago Board of Trade
Contract Size	USD 100,000.00
Tick Size	One half of 1/32 of one point
Tick Value	USD 15.625
Quoted in	points

OPTIONS

Contract Size	One futures contract
Tick Size	1/64 of one point
Tick Value	USD 15.625

Continuous | Sunday – Friday: 5:00 p.m. – 4:00 p.m. with a one hour break from 4:00 p.m. to 5:00 p.m. every day except Friday, which closes at 4:00 p.m.
Central Standard Time - Chicago

TRADING TIPS
The most followed metric of the US bond market. It is heavily traded by investors around the world and is viewed as a safe bet during turbulent times. Physical delivery.

LIQUIDITY   LEVERAGE   VOLATILITY
High   High   Low

BOND

5-Year T-Note

United States of America

5-year Treasury Notes have a $100,000 face value. You receive interest 6% monthly and the face value on maturity. Now all electronic, and purchasable at auction in $100 denominations. The cornerstone of the US economy.

FUTURES

Symbol	ZF
Electronic Venue	CME-CBT
Exchange Name	Chicago Board of Trade
Contract Size	USD 100,000.00
Tick Size	One quarter of 1/32
Tick Value	USD 7.8125
Quoted in	points

OPTIONS

Contract Size	One futures contract
Tick Size	One half of 1/64
Tick Value	USD 7.8125

Continuous | Sunday – Friday: 5:00 p.m. – 4:00 p.m. with a one hour break from 4:00 p.m. to 5:00 p.m. every day except Friday, which closes at 4:00 p.m.
Central Standard Time - Chicago

TRADING TIPS

Are you looking to bet on the shape of the yield curve? Don't look any further. An important asset on every bond manager's portfolio. Physical delivery.

LIQUIDITY   **LEVERAGE**   **VOLATILITY**
High   High   Low

BOND
2-Year T-Note
United States of America

2-year Treasury Notes have a $200,000 face value. You receive interest 6% monthly and the face value on maturity. Now all electronic, they can be sold and bought at auction in $100 denominations.

FUTURES

Symbol	ZT
Electronic Venue	CME-CBT
Exchange Name	Chicago Board of Trade
Contract Size	USD 200,000.00
Tick Size	One quarter of 1/32
Tick Value	USD 15.625
Quoted in	points

OPTIONS

Contract Size	One futures contract
Tick Size	One half of 1/64
Tick Value	USD 15.625

Continuous | Sunday – Friday: 5:00 p.m. – 4:00 p.m. with a one hour break from 4:00 p.m. to 5:00 p.m. every day except Friday, which closes at 4:00 p.m.
Central Standard Time - Chicago

TRADING TIPS

Short-term rate instruments should be better left to professionals. Not as popular with day-traders as the 10-year because of smaller percentage point moves. Physical delivery.

LIQUIDITY   LEVERAGE   VOLATILITY
High   High   Low

BOND

Ten-Year Government of Canada Bond
Canada

A 100,000 Canadian Dollars nominal value of Government of Canada Bond bearing a 6% notional coupon.

FUTURES

Symbol	CGB
Electronic Venue	MFE
Exchange Name	Montréal Exchange
Contract Size	CAD 100,000.00
Tick Size	0.01
Tick Value	CAD 10
Quoted in	points

OPTIONS

Contract Size	One futures contract
Tick Size	0.005
Tick Value	CAD 5

Day Session | Monday to Friday: 6:00 a.m. – 8:05 a.m. & 8:20 – 3:00 p.m. & 3:06 p.m. – 4:00 p.m.
Eastern Standard Time – Montreal

TRADING TIPS

Sensitive to oil prices. Physical delivery.

LIQUIDITY	**LEVERAGE**	**VOLATILITY**
Medium	High	Low

BOND

Two-Year Government of Canada Bond
Canada

A 200,000 Canadian Dollars nominal value of Government of Canada Bond bearing a 6% notional coupon.

FUTURES

Symbol	CGZ
Electronic Venue	MFE
Exchange Name	Montréal Exchange
Contract Size	CAD 200,000.00
Tick Size	0.005
Tick Value	CAD 10
Quoted in	points

Day Session | Monday to Friday: 6:00 a.m. – 4:00 p.m. Eastern Standard Time – Montreal

TRADING TIPS

Not particularly suitable for day-trading due to low volume and small price moves. Physical delivery.

LIQUIDITY LEVERAGE VOLATILITY

Low   High   Low

BOND

Five-Year Government of Canada Bond
Canada

A 100,000 Canadian Dollars nominal value of Government of Canada Bond bearing a 6% notional coupon.

FUTURES

Symbol	CGF
Electronic Venue	MFE
Exchange Name	Montréal Exchange
Contract Size	CAD 100,000.00
Tick Size	0.01
Tick Value	CAD 10
Quoted in	points

Day Session | Monday to Friday: 6:00 a.m. – 4:00 p.m.
Eastern Standard Time – Montreal

TRADING TIPS

More active than the 2-year Canadian Bond but still not liquid enough for day trading. Physical delivery.

LIQUIDITY	**LEVERAGE**	**VOLATILITY**
Low	High	Low

BOND

Long Gilt
Great Britain

Bonds issued by the UK Government. They are the safest of all investments. Holders of mature gilts receive the final coupon payment plus the principal. Maturity of 8 3/4 to 13 years from the 1st calendar day of the delivery month.

FUTURES

Symbol	R
Electronic Venue	ICE
Exchange Name	ICE Futures - Europe
Contract Size	GBP 100,000.00
Tick Size	0.01
Tick Value	GBP 10
Quoted in	per GBP100 nominal

Day Session | Monday to Friday: 8:00 a.m. – 6:00 p.m. Greenwich Mean Time - London

TRADING TIPS

Gilts are the UK equivalent to US Securities. The term "long" indicates the maturity of the issue. Physical delivery.

LIQUIDITY	**LEVERAGE**	**VOLATILITY**
High	High	Low

BOND

Short Gilt

Great Britain

Bonds issued by the UK Government. They are the safest of all investments. Holders of mature gilts receive the final coupon payment plus the principal. Short Gilts mature in 18 to 39 months and bear a coupon of 3%.

FUTURES

Symbol	G
Electronic Venue	ICE
Exchange Name	ICE Futures - Europe
Contract Size	GBP 100,000.00
Tick Size	0.01
Tick Value	GBP 10
Quoted in	per GBP100 nominal

Day Session | Monday to Friday: 8:00 a.m. – 6:00 p.m. Greenwich Mean Time - London

TRADING TIPS

Short-term debt instrument with low volume and high fluctuations of open interest. Most trading activity is made over the counter. Physical delivery.

LIQUIDITY   LEVERAGE   VOLATILITY
Low   High   Low

BOND

Euro-Oat
France

Introduced in 2012 this is a long term debt instrument with Futures in French Government Bonds. It bears a coupon of 6%.

FUTURES

Symbol	FOAT
Electronic Venue	EUREX
Exchange Name	Eurex
Contract Size	100,000.00 EUR
Tick Size	0.01
Tick Value	EUR 10
Quoted in	Percentage of par value

Day Session | Monday to Friday: 8:00 a.m. – 7:00 p.m. Central European Time - Frankfurt

TRADING TIPS

The latest addition to the European bond futures family. The French contract is structured similarly to its German and Italian counterparts enabling efficient spread strategies. Physical delivery.

LIQUIDITY   LEVERAGE   VOLATILITY

High   High   Low

Category 3 - Currencies

CURRENCIES

EUR/USD
United States of America

A futures contract to exchange one currency for another at a specified date in the future at a price (exchange rate) that is fixed on the purchase date. Buy the EUR/USD future when you expect the Euro to appreciate against the US Dollar.

FUTURES

Symbol	6E
Electronic Venue	GLOBEX
Exchange Name	Chicago Mercantile Exchange
Contract Size	EUR 125,000.00
Tick Size	0.0001
Tick Value	USD 12.5
Quoted in	USD/EUR

OPTIONS

Contract Size	One futures contract
Tick Size	0.0001
Tick Value	USD 12.5

Continuous | Sunday to Friday: 5:00 p.m. – 4:00 p.m. with a one hour break from 4:00 p.m. to 5:00 every day except Friday, which closes at 4:00 p.m.
Central Standard Time - Chicago

TRADING TIPS

Euro FX is the undisputed leader in currency trading with billions of dollars changing hands every single day. Physical delivery.

LIQUIDITY	**LEVERAGE**	**VOLATILITY**
High	High	High

CURRENCIES

GBP/USD

United States of America

A futures contract to exchange one currency for another at a specified date in the future at a price (exchange rate) that is fixed on the purchase date. Buy the GBP/USD future when you expect the British Pound to appreciate against the US Dollar.

FUTURES

Symbol	6B
Electronic Venue	GLOBEX
Exchange Name	Chicago Mercantile Exchange
Contract Size	GBP 62,500.00
Tick Size	0.0001
Tick Value	USD 6.25
Quoted in	cents/GBP

OPTIONS

Contract Size	One futures contract
Tick Size	0.0001
Tick Value	USD 6.25

Continuous | Sunday to Friday: 5:00 p.m. – 4:00 p.m. with a one hour break from 4:00 p.m. to 5:00 every day except Friday, which closes at 4:00 p.m.
Central Standard Time - Chicago

TRADING TIPS

Also known as "cable", the GBP/USD exchange rate is one of the majors. It enjoys sharp price fluctuations and attracts a great deal of speculators. Physical delivery.

LIQUIDITY   LEVERAGE   VOLATILITY

High   High   Medium

CURRENCIES

JPY/USD
United States of America

A futures contract to exchange one currency for another at a specified date in the future at a price (exchange rate) that is fixed on the purchase date. Buy the JPY/USD future when you expect the Japanese Yen to appreciate against the US Dollar.

FUTURES

Symbol	6J
Electronic Venue	GLOBEX
Exchange Name	Chicago Mercantile Exchange
Contract Size	JPY 12,500,000.00
Tick Size	0.000001
Tick Value	USD 12.5
Quoted in	cents/100 JPY

OPTIONS

Contract Size	One futures contract
Tick Size	0.000001
Tick Value	USD 12.5

Continuous | Sunday to Friday: 5:00 p.m. – 4:00 p.m. with a one hour break from 4:00 p.m. to 5:00 every day except Friday, which closes at 4:00 p.m.
Central Standard Time - Chicago.

TRADING TIPS

Stimulus from the Bank of Japan in relation to US yields influences price moves. So does the Tankan Manufacturing report that is released quarterly. Physical delivery.

LIQUIDITY	**LEVERAGE**	**VOLATILITY**
High	High	Low

CURRENCIES

EUR/JPY
United States of America

A futures contract to exchange one currency for another at a specified date in the future at a price (exchange rate) that is fixed on the purchase date. Buy the EUR/JPY future when you expect the Euro to appreciate against the Japanese Yen.

FUTURES

Symbol	RY
Electronic Venue	GLOBEX
Exchange Name	Chicago Mercantile Exchange
Contract Size	EUR 125,000.00
Tick Size	0.01
Tick Value	JPY 1250
Quoted in	JPY/EUR

OPTIONS

Contract Size	One futures contract
Tick Size	0.01
Tick Value	JPY 1250

Continuous | Sunday to Friday: 5:00 p.m. – 4:00 p.m. with a one hour break from 4:00 p.m. to 5:00 every day except Friday, which closes at 4:00 p.m.
Central Standard Time - Chicago

TRADING TIPS

EUR/JPY's price range is influenced mainly by the moves of the major currencies. Stop loss orders should be treated with care due to low volume. Physical delivery.

LIQUIDITY	**LEVERAGE**	**VOLATILITY**
Low	High	Medium

CURRENCIES

EUR/GBP
United States of America

A futures contract to exchange one currency for another at a specified date in the future at a price (exchange rate) that is fixed on the purchase date. Buy the EUR/GBP future when you expect the Euro to appreciate against the British Pound.

FUTURES

Symbol	RP
Electronic Venue	GLOBEX
Exchange Name	Chicago Mercantile Exchange
Contract Size	EUR 125,000.00
Tick Size	0.00005
Tick Value	GBP 6.25
Quoted in	GBP/EUR

OPTIONS

Contract Size	One futures contract
Tick Size	0.00005
Tick Value	GBP 6.25

Continuous | Sunday to Friday: 5:00 p.m. – 4:00 p.m. with a one hour break from 4:00 p.m. to 5:00 every day except Friday, which closes at 4:00 p.m.
Central Standard Time - Chicago

TRADING TIPS

As a cross currency, the EUR/GBP's price range is influenced mainly by the moves of the majors. Physical delivery.

LIQUIDITY	**LEVERAGE**	**VOLATILITY**
Low	High	Medium

CURRENCIES

EUR/CHF
United States of America

A futures contract to exchange one currency for another at a specified date in the future at a price (exchange rate) that is fixed on the purchase date. Buy the EUR/CHF future when you expect EUR to appreciate against the CHF.

FUTURES

Symbol	RF
Electronic Venue	GLOBEX
Exchange Name	Chicago Mercantile Exchange
Contract Size	EUR 125,000.00
Tick Size	0.0001
Tick Value	CHF 12.5
Quoted in	CHF/EUR

OPTIONS

Contract Size	One futures contract
Tick Size	0.0001
Tick Value	CHF 12.5

Continuous | Sunday to Friday: 5:00 p.m. – 4:00 p.m. with a one hour break from 4:00 p.m. to 5:00 every day except Friday, which closes at 4:00 p.m.
Central Standard Time - Chicago

TRADING TIPS

This is a low-volume cross. Physical delivery.

LIQUIDITY	**LEVERAGE**	**VOLATILITY**
Low	High	Low

CURRENCIES

AUD/USD
United States of America

A futures contract to exchange one currency for another at a specified date in the future at a price (exchange rate) that is fixed on the purchase date. Buy the AUD/USD future when you expect the Australian Dollar to appreciate against the US Dollar.

FUTURES

Symbol	6A
Electronic Venue	GLOBEX
Exchange Name	Chicago Mercantile Exchange
Contract Size	AUD 100,000.00
Tick Size	0.0001
Tick Value	USD 10
Quoted in	cents/AUD

OPTIONS

Contract Size	One futures contract
Tick Size	0.0001
Tick Value	USD 10

Continuous | Sunday to Friday: 5:00 p.m. – 4:00 p.m. with a one hour break from 4:00 p.m. to 5:00 every day except Friday, which closes at 4:00 p.m.
Central Standard Time - Chicago

TRADING TIPS

The Australian Dollar is considered a "Risk On" asset. Correlates with commodity prices and growth rates in Asia, especially China. Physical delivery.

LIQUIDITY   LEVERAGE   VOLATILITY
High   High   Medium

CURRENCIES

CHF/USD

United States of America

A futures contract to exchange one currency for another at a specified date in the future at a price (exchange rate) that is fixed on the purchase date. Buy the CHF/USD future when you expect the Swiss Franc to appreciate against the US Dollar.

FUTURES

Symbol	6S
Electronic Venue	GLOBEX
Exchange Name	Chicago Mercantile Exchange
Contract Size	CHF 125.000
Tick Size	0.0001
Tick Value	USD 12.5
Quoted in	cents/CHF

OPTIONS

Contract Size	One futures contract
Tick Size	0.0001
Tick Value	USD 12.5

Continuous | Sunday to Friday: 5:00 p.m. – 4:00 p.m. with a one hour break from 4:00 p.m. to 5:00 every day except Friday, which closes at 4:00 p.m.
Central Standard Time - Chicago

TRADING TIPS

Traders call this FX spot rate the "Swissie". As a famous "Risk Off" exchange rate, the CHF/USD future contract is considered a safe haven for the most part. Physical delivery.

LIQUIDITY	**LEVERAGE**	**VOLATILITY**
High	Medium	Medium

CURRENCIES

E-mini EUR/USD
United States of America

A futures contract to exchange one currency for another at a specified date in the future at a price (exchange rate) that is fixed on the purchase date. Buy the Mini EUR/USD future when you expect the Euro to appreciate against the US Dollar.

FUTURES

Symbol	E7
Electronic Venue	GLOBEX
Exchange Name	Chicago Mercantile Exchange
Contract Size	EUR 62,500.00
Tick Size	0.0001
Tick Value	USD 6.25
Quoted in	USD/EUR

Continuous | Sunday to Friday: 5:00 p.m. – 4:00 p.m. with a one hour break from 4:00 p.m. to 5:00 every day except Friday, which closes at 4:00 p.m.
Central Standard Time - Chicago

TRADING TIPS

Half the size of the Euro FX contract, the E-mini EUR/USD is sometimes used as a hedge against the large-size contract in order to reduce initial exposure by half. Not as liquid as its big brother, so stop loss orders should be treated with care. Physical delivery.

LIQUIDITY   LEVERAGE   VOLATILITY
Low   High   Medium

CURRENCIES

E-mini JPY/USD
United States of America

A futures contract to exchange one currency for another at a specified date in the future at a price (exchange rate) that is fixed on the purchase date. Buy the mini JPY/USD future when you expect the Japanese Yen to appreciate against the US Dollar.

FUTURES

Symbol	J7
Electronic Venue	GLOBEX
Exchange Name	Chicago Mercantile Exchange
Contract Size	JPY 6,250,000.00
Tick Size	0.000001
Tick Value	USD 6.25
Quoted in	cents/100 JPY

Continuous | Sunday to Friday: 5:00 p.m. – 4:00 p.m. with a one hour break from 4:00 p.m. to 5:00 every day except Friday, which closes at 4:00 p.m.
Central Standard Time - Chicago

TRADING TIPS

Low liquidity and wide bid/ask spreads do not make it ideal for day-trading. Physical delivery.

LIQUIDITY   LEVERAGE   VOLATILITY
Low   High   Low

CURRENCIES

NZD/USD
United States of America

A futures contract to exchange one currency for another at a specified date in the future at a price (exchange rate) that is fixed on the purchase date. Buy the NZD/USD future when you expect the New Zealand Dollar to appreciate against the US Dollar.

FUTURES

Symbol	6N
Electronic Venue	GLOBEX
Exchange Name	Chicago Mercantile Exchange
Contract Size	NZD 100,000.00
Tick Size	0.0001
Tick Value	USD 10
Quoted in	cents/NZD

OPTIONS

Contract Size	One futures contract
Tick Size	0.0001
Tick Value	USD 10

Continuous | Sunday to Friday: 5:00 p.m. – 4:00 p.m. with a 1 hour break from 4:00 p.m. to 5:00 every day except Friday, which closes at 4:00 p.m.
Central Standard Time - Chicago

TRADING TIPS

China, commodities and dairy prices are three important factors influencing the "kiwi" exchange rate. Physical delivery.

LIQUIDITY	**LEVERAGE**	**VOLATILITY**
Medium	High	Medium

CURRENCIES

MXN/USD

United States of America

A futures contract to exchange one currency for another at a specified date in the future at a price (exchange rate) that is fixed on the purchase date. Buy the MXN/USD future when you expect the Mexican Peso to appreciate against the US Dollar.

FUTURES

Symbol	6M
Electronic Venue	GLOBEX
Exchange Name	Chicago Mercantile Exchange
Contract Size	MXN 500,000.00
Tick Size	0.000025
Tick Value	USD 12.5
Quoted in	cents/MXN

OPTIONS

Contract Size	One futures contract
Tick Size	0.000025
Tick Value	USD 12.5

Continuous | Sunday to Friday: 5:00 p.m. – 4:00 p.m. with a one hour break from 4:00 p.m. to 5:00 every day except Friday, which closes at 4:00 p.m.
Central Standard Time - Chicago

TRADING TIPS

One of the most heavily traded and transparent exchange rates in the Latin American region. Negatively correlates with the price of oil. Physical delivery.

LIQUIDITY	**LEVERAGE**	**VOLATILITY**
Medium	Low	Medium

CURRENCIES

Micro EUR/USD
United States of America

A futures contract to exchange one currency for another at a specified date in the future at a price (exchange rate) that is fixed on the purchase date. Buy the Micro EUR/USD future when you expect the Euro to appreciate against the US Dollar.

FUTURES

Symbol	M6E
Electronic Venue	GLOBEX
Exchange Name	Chicago Mercantile Exchange
Contract Size	EUR 12,500.00
Tick Size	0.0001
Tick Value	USD 1.25
Quoted in	USD/EUR

Continuous | Sunday to Friday: 5:00 p.m. – 4:00 p.m. with a one hour break from 4:00 p.m. to 5:00 every day except Friday, which closes at 4:00 p.m.
Central Standard Time - Chicago

TRADING TIPS

The smallest member of the EUR/USD family of futures. The Micro EUR/USD is liquid enough for intraday transactions but the notional size is small. Physical delivery.

LIQUIDITY	**LEVERAGE**	**VOLATILITY**
Low	High	Medium

CURRENCIES

CAD/USD
United States of America

A futures contract to exchange one currency for another at a specified date in the future at a price (exchange rate) that is fixed on the purchase date. Buy the CAD/USD future when you expect the Canadian Dollar to appreciate against the US Dollar.

FUTURES

Symbol	6C
Electronic Venue	GLOBEX
Exchange Name	Chicago Mercantile Exchange
Contract Size	CAD 100,000.00
Tick Size	0.0001
Tick Value	USD 10
Quoted in	cents/CAD

OPTIONS

Contract Size	One futures contract
Tick Size	0.0001
Tick Value	USD 10

Continuous |Sunday to Friday: 5:00 p.m. – 4:00 p.m. with a one hour break from 4:00 p.m. to 5:00 every day except Friday, which closes at 4:00 p.m.
Central Standard Time - Chicago

TRADING TIPS

Canada's role as a major commodity exporter exposes its currency to high fluctuations and to the risk of a fall in oil prices. Physical delivery.

LIQUIDITY   LEVERAGE   VOLATILITY

High   Medium   Low

Category 4 - Emissions

EMISSIONS

ICE - Emissions
Great Britain

ICE ECX EUA or EU allowances are entitlements to emit one ton of carbon dioxide equivalent gas. It is the most liquid, pan-European platform for carbon emissions trading.

FUTURES

Symbol	ECF
Electronic Venue	ICE
Exchange Name	ICE Futures - Europe
Contract Size	1,000.00 Metric Tons
Tick Size	0.01
Tick Value	EUR 10
Quoted in	EUR/MT

OPTIONS

Contract Size	One futures contract
Tick Size	0.01
Tick Value	EUR 10

Day Session | Monday to Friday: 7:00 a.m. – 5:00 p.m. Greenwich Mean Time - London

TRADING TIPS

The world's leading contract in carbon trading that complies with EU Emissions Trading System. Suitable for the airline industry, power groups and manufacturers. Physical delivery.

LIQUIDITY	**LEVERAGE**	**VOLATILITY**
Medium	Low	High

Category 5 - Energy

ENERGY

Light Sweet Crude Oil
United States of America

West Texas Intermediate (WTI): think oil price benchmark and you're thinking of Texas Light Sweet. Low density, low sulfur petroleum refined around the Midwest and Gulf Coast. Easy to process and especially suitable for making gasoline.

FUTURES

Symbol	CL
Electronic Venue	GLOBEX
Exchange Name	New York Mercantile Exchange
Contract Size	1,000.00 Barrels
Tick Size	0.01
Tick Value	USD 10
Quoted in	USD/barrel

OPTIONS

Contract Size	One futures contract
Tick Size	0.01
Tick Value	USD 10

Continuous | Sunday to Friday: 6:00 p.m. – 5:00 p.m. with a 60 min break from 5:00 p.m. to 6:00 p.m. every day except Friday, which closes at 5:00 p.m.
Eastern Standard Time - New York

TRADING TIPS

The fuel of choice for the world's automobiles. Structural anomalies between WTI and Brent oil may produce arbitrage opportunities for speculation. Physical delivery.

LIQUIDITY	**LEVERAGE**	**VOLATILITY**
High	Low	High

ENERGY

Henry Hub Natural Gas
United States of America

A hydrocarbon gas mixture and a major source of electricity and heat generation. The Henry Hub is located in Louisiana's Wetlands and has served as the pricing benchmark for the North American natural gas market since 1990. It is the delivery point for Nymex futures contracts.

FUTURES

Symbol	NG
Electronic Venue	GLOBEX
Exchange Name	New York Mercantile Exchange
Contract Size	10,000.00 MMBtu
Tick Size	0.001
Tick Value	USD 10
Quoted in	

OPTIONS

Contract Size	One futures contract
Tick Size	0.001
Tick Value	USD 10

Continuous | Sunday to Friday: 6:00 p.m. – 5:00 p.m. with a 60 min break from 5:00 p.m. to 6:00 p.m. every day except Friday, which closes at 5:00 p.m.
Eastern Standard Time - New York

TRADING TIPS

Watch for weather patterns and stockpiles. Expectations for harsh winters skew prices to the upside. Make no mistake about it; deep pocket traders make it one of the most risky energy markets. Physical delivery.

LIQUIDITY   LEVERAGE   VOLATILITY
High   Low   High

ENERGY

ICE Brent Crude
Great Britain

Brent Crude: sourced from the North Sea and refined in Northwest Europe, it serves as the leading global price benchmark for Atlantic basin crude oils. Price differences between Brent and Sweet Light drive the trading activities of arbitrageurs and speculators.

FUTURES

Symbol	BRN
Electronic Venue	ICE
Exchange Name	ICE Futures - Europe
Contract Size	1,000.00 Barrels
Tick Size	0.01
Tick Value	USD 10
Quoted in	USD/barrel

OPTIONS

Contract Size	One futures contract
Tick Size	0.01
Tick Value	USD 10

Continuous | Sunday to Friday: 8:00 p.m. – 6:00 p.m. with a 2 hour break from 6:00 p.m. to 8:00 p.m. every day except Friday, which closes at 6:00 p.m.
Eastern Standard Time - New York

TRADING TIPS

Differences in crude properties between Brent and WTI as well as variations in supply and demand explain the difference in prices, according to the US Energy Information Administration. Cash settled.

LIQUIDITY	**LEVERAGE**	**VOLATILITY**
High	Low	High

ENERGY

E-mini Natural Gas
United States of America

(Mini) Natural Gas is a hydrocarbon gas mixture and a major source of electricity and heat generation. The Henry Hub is located in Louisiana's Wetlands and has served as the pricing benchmark for the North American natural gas market since 1990. It is the delivery point for Nymex futures contracts.

FUTURES

Symbol	QG
Electronic Venue	GLOBEX
Exchange Name	New York Mercantile Exchange
Contract Size	2,500.00 MMBtu
Tick Size	0.005
Tick Value	USD 12.5
Quoted in	

Continuous | Sunday to Friday: 6:00 p.m. – 5:00 p.m. with a 60 min break from 5:00 p.m. to 6:00 p.m. every day except Friday, which closes at 5:00 p.m.
Eastern Standard Time - New York

TRADING TIPS

A cash settled contract with small notional size and relatively low volume.

LIQUIDITY	**LEVERAGE**	**VOLATILITY**
Medium	Low	High

ENERGY

E-mini Crude Oil
United States of America

(Mini) West Texas Intermediate (WTI): think oil price benchmark and you're thinking of Texas Light Sweet. Low density, Low sulfur petroleum refined around the Midwest and Gulf Coast. Structural anomalies between WTI and Brent oil may produce arbitrage opportunities for speculation.

FUTURES

Symbol	QM
Electronic Venue	GLOBEX
Exchange Name	New York Mercantile Exchange
Contract Size	500.00 Barrels
Tick Size	0.025
Tick Value	USD 12.5
Quoted in	

Continuous | Sunday to Friday: 6:00 p.m. – 5:00 p.m. with a 60 min break from 5:00 p.m. to 6:00 p.m. every day except Friday, which closes at 5:00 p.m.
Eastern Standard Time - New York

TRADING TIPS

A cash settled contract with small notional size and low volume.

LIQUIDITY	**LEVERAGE**	**VOLATILITY**
Medium	Low	High

Category 6 - Equity Indices

EQUITY INDICES

DAX
Germany

DAX Index comprises 30 Blue Chip German companies that trade on the Frankfurt Stock Exchange. International investors follow it closely because its constituents generate most of their sales abroad. The choice of professionals and risk takers.

FUTURES

Symbol	FDAX
Electronic Venue	EUREX
Exchange Name	Eurex
Contract Size	EUR 25.00 x Index
Tick Size	0.5
Tick Value	EUR 12.5
Quoted in	Index points

Day Session | Monday to Friday: 7:50 a.m. – 10:00 p.m. Central European Time - Frankfurt

OPTIONS

Contract Size	EUR 5.00 x Index
Tick Size	0.1
Tick Value	EUR 0.5

Day Session | Monday to Friday: 8:50 a.m. – 5:30 p.m. Central European Time - Europe/Frankfurt

TRADING TIPS

The export-based nature of Germany has made the DAX an important global benchmark. It has a high sensitivity to the EUR/USD exchange rate. Cash settled.

LIQUIDITY	**LEVERAGE**	**VOLATILITY**
High	Low	High

EQUITY INDICES

EuroStoxx 50
Germany

The leading Blue-chip index for the Eurozone with 50 stocks from 12 countries. It serves as the underlying instrument for a wide range of investment products such as Exchange Traded Funds (ETF), Futures, Options, and structured products worldwide.

FUTURES

Symbol	FESX
Electronic Venue	EUREX
Exchange Name	Eurex
Contract Size	EUR 10.00 x Index
Tick Size	1
Tick Value	EUR 10
Quoted in	Index points

Day Session | Monday to Friday: 7:50 a.m. – 10:00 p.m. Central European Time - Frankfurt

OPTIONS

Contract Size	EUR 10.00 x Index
Tick Size	0.1
Tick Value	EUR 1

Day Session | Monday to Friday: 8:50 a.m. – 5:30 p.m. Central European Time - Frankfurt

TRADING TIPS
A pan European index with an emphasis on the financial sector. A well-structured index designed for professionals and retail investors alike. Cash settled.

LIQUIDITY	**LEVERAGE**	**VOLATILITY**
High	Low	High

EQUITY INDICES

SMI
Switzerland

Switzerland's most important stock market index, made up of 20 of the largest and most liquid large and mid-cap stocks. You can hedge the vast majority of the total capitalization of Swiss equities with its futures contracts.

FUTURES

Symbol	FSMI
Electronic Venue	EUREX
Exchange Name	Eurex
Contract Size	CHF 10.00 x Index
Tick Size	1
Tick Value	CHF 10
Quoted in	Index points

Day Session | Monday to Friday: 7:50 a.m. – 10:00 p.m. Central European Time - Frankfurt

OPTIONS

Contract Size	CHF 10.00 x Index
Tick Size	0.1
Tick Value	CHF 1

Day Session | Monday to Friday: 8:50 a.m. – 5:20 p.m. Central European Time - Frankfurt

TRADING TIPS

Monetary stability, low public debt and low unemployment make the Swiss market one of the safest in the world. Not a thrill to trade but it does have its moments. Cash settled.

LIQUIDITY	**LEVERAGE**	**VOLATILITY**
High	Low	Medium

EQUITY INDICES

BIST 30
Turkey

BIST 30 Index (formerly known as ISE National-30 Index) is actively followed by international investors. Its 30 constituents include banks, conglomerates, retail, petrochemicals, telecoms, transportation and others.

FUTURES

Symbol	111
Electronic Venue	TURKDEX
Exchange Name	Turkish Derivatives Exchange
Contract Size	TRY 100.00 x Index
Tick Size	0.025
Tick Value	TRY 2.5
Quoted in	Index points

Day Session | Monday to Friday: 9:10 a.m. – 5:45 p.m.
Eastern European Time - Istanbul

TRADING TIPS

Turkey has a dynamic and export-driven economy and is one of the leading emerging markets in the world. Wild swings in the Turkish lira should be watched carefully. Cash settled.

LIQUIDITY	**LEVERAGE**	**VOLATILITY**
High	Low	High

EQUITY INDICES

E-mini Dow ($5)
United States of America

Dow Jones Industrial Average, Dow 30 or Dow is the most widely recognized index globally and the most closely watched benchmark index in the US. The 30 constituents are price weighted so high value stocks make it move.

FUTURES

Symbol	YM
Electronic Venue	CME CBT
Exchange Name	Chicago Board of Trade
Contract Size	USD 5.00 x Index
Tick Size	1
Tick Value	USD 5
Quoted in	Index points

OPTIONS

Contract Size	One futures contract
Tick Size	1
Tick Value	USD 5

Continuous | Sunday to Friday: 5:00 p.m. – 4:00 p.m. with a 15 min break from 3:15 p.m. to 3:30 p.m. and a 60 min break from 4:00 p.m. to 5:00 p.m. every day except Friday, which closes at 4:00 p.m.
Central Standard Time - Chicago

TRADING TIPS

Once a bellwether of the US economy, the Dow Jones has now passed on this title to the S&P 500. It remains a very important benchmark and a highly attractive futures market. Cash settled.

LIQUIDITY	**LEVERAGE**	**VOLATILITY**
High	Medium	Medium

EQUITY INDICES

Mini S&P 500
United States of America

The S&P 500 Index is the world's most widely followed benchmark of stock market performance. It is a bellwether for the US economy. Its 500 large-capitalization stocks include US and non-US companies that are traded on the NYSE, AMEX and the NASDAQ.

FUTURES

Symbol	ES
Electronic Venue	GLOBEX
Exchange Name	Chicago Mercantile Exchange
Contract Size	USD 50.00 x Index
Tick Size	0.25
Tick Value	USD 12.5
Quoted in	Index points

OPTIONS

Contract Size	One futures contract
Tick Size	0.05
Tick Value	USD 2.5

Continuous | Sunday to Friday: 5:00 p.m. – 4:00 p.m. with a 15 min break from 3:15 p.m. to 3:30 p.m. and a 60 min break from 4:00 p.m. to 5:00 p.m. every day except Friday, which closes at 4:00 p.m.
Central Standard Time - Chicago

TRADING TIPS

The ultimate stock index of the US market. It attracts all sorts of participants including algo hedge funds, mutual funds, pension funds and retail investors. Cash settled.

LIQUIDITY	LEVERAGE	VOLATILITY
High	Medium	Medium

EQUITY INDICES

Mini NASDAQ 100
United States of America

The Nasdaq-100 represents international issues listed on the NASDAQ Stock Market including the largest from the US but excluding financials. The index is based on a modified market capitalization. Sectors include computer hardware and software, telecoms, trade and biotechnology.

FUTURES

Symbol	NQ
Electronic Venue	GLOBEX
Exchange Name	Chicago Mercantile Exchange
Contract Size	USD 20.00 x Index
Tick Size	0.25
Tick Value	USD 5
Quoted in	Index points

OPTIONS

Contract Size	One futures contract
Tick Size	0.05
Tick Value	USD 1

Continuous | Sunday to Friday: 5:00 p.m. – 4:00 p.m. with a 15 min break from 3:15 p.m. to 3:30 p.m. and a 60 min break from 4:00 p.m. to 5:00 p.m. every day except Friday, which closes at 4:00 p.m.
Central Standard Time - Chicago

TRADING TIPS

NASDAQ's entrepreneurial and high-tech nature makes it one of the most popular indices and, some say a leading indicator of the entire US market. Cash settled.

LIQUIDITY	**LEVERAGE**	**VOLATILITY**
High	High	Medium

EQUITY INDICES

Mini Russell 2000
United States of America

The Russell 2000 is a benchmark for US small caps. Covers 8% of the total capitalization on the Russell 3000 comprising the bottom 2000 stocks. You'll be keeping a careful eye here as returns can differ significantly from the mainstream indices.

FUTURES

Symbol	TF
Electronic Venue	ICE
Exchange Name	ICE Futures US Indices
Contract Size	USD 100.00 x Index
Tick Size	0.1
Tick Value	USD 10
Quoted in	Index points

OPTIONS

Contract Size	One futures contract
Tick Size	0.05
Tick Value	USD 5

Continuous | Sunday to Friday: 6:00 p.m. − 6:00 p.m. with a 2 hour break from 6:00 p.m. to 8:00 p.m. every weekday except Friday, which closes at 6:00 p.m.
Eastern Standard Time - New York

TRADING TIPS

A common diversification play. The backbone of the US economy can be found here. Cash settled.

LIQUIDITY	**LEVERAGE**	**VOLATILITY**
High	Medium	Medium

Equity Indices

Nikkei 225
United States of America

The Nikkei 225 (Dollar) was initiated in 1950. A price weighted index and the most widely recognized index in Japan. Calculated from a selection of 225 domestic common stocks listed on Tokyo Stock Exchange, reviewed annually and reshuffled usually in October.

FUTURES

Symbol	NKD
Electronic Venue	GLOBEX
Exchange Name	Chicago Mercantile Exchange
Contract Size	USD 5.00 x Index
Tick Size	5
Tick Value	USD 25
Quoted in	Index points

Continuous | Sunday to Friday: 5:00 p.m. − 4:00 p.m. with a 60 min break from 4:00 p.m. to 5:00 p.m. every day except Friday, which closes at 4:00 p.m.
Central Standard Time - Chicago

TRADING TIPS

The dollar-denominated Nikkei 225 Index caters to the needs of investors in the Western hemisphere. A relatively low volume market but in a convenient time frame for non-Asia based investors. Cash settled.

LIQUIDITY	**LEVERAGE**	**VOLATILITY**
Low	Medium	Medium

EQUITY INDICES

FTSE 100
Great Britain

The FTSE 100 measures the performance of 100 of the largest UK listed companies that account for about 80% of the London Stock Exchange. Represents companies from the Oil & Gas, Banking, Telecoms, Pharmaceuticals, Tobacco, Beverages, Mining and Energy sectors.

FUTURES

Symbol	Z
Electronic Venue	ICE
Exchange Name	ICE Futures - Europe
Contract Size	GBP 10.00 x Index
Tick Size	0.5
Tick Value	GBP 5
Quoted in	Index points

Day Session | Monday to Friday: 1:00 a.m. – 9:00 p.m.

OPTIONS

Contract Size	GBP 10.00 x Index
Tick Size	0.5
Tick Value	GBP 5

Day Session | Monday to Friday: 8:00 a.m. – 4:30 p.m. Greenwich Mean Time - London

TRADING TIPS

The bellwether of the UK economy and a solid indicator of international trade. Cyclical stocks take almost half of the capitalization. Cash settled.

LIQUIDITY	LEVERAGE	VOLATILITY
High	Medium	Medium

EQUITY INDICES
IBEX
Spain

IBEX 35 are the most liquid stocks on the Madrid stock exchange. Weightings are not capped. Changes in composition of constituents happen on 1st of July and January.

FUTURES

Symbol	FIE
Electronic Venue	MEFF-MADRID
Exchange Name	Meff Renta Variable (Madrid)
Contract Size	EUR 10.00 x Index
Tick Size	1
Tick Value	EUR 10
Quoted in	Index points

Day Session | Monday to Friday: 9:00 a.m. – 8:00 p.m. Central European Time - Madrid

TRADING TIPS

The benchmark of the Spanish market. A large weight is given on the banking sector. Cash settled.

LIQUIDITY   LEVERAGE   VOLATILITY

Low   Low   High

EQUITY INDICES
Mini FTSE MIB
Italy

FTSE MIB is the benchmark index for the Italian stock market. It measures the performance of 40 most liquid and capitalized stocks in the Italian market and captures approximately 80% of the country's market capitalization.

FUTURES

Symbol	MINI
Electronic Venue	MIFE
Exchange Name	Borsa Italiana (IDEM)
Contract Size	EUR 1.00 x Index
Tick Size	5
Tick Value	EUR 5
Quoted in	Index points

Day Session | Monday to Friday: 9:00 a.m. to 5:50 p.m. Central European Time - Rome

TRADING TIPS

Half the size of the FTSE MIB, the mini MIB is designed primarily for retail investors. Daily volume measured in number of lots can sometimes exceed open interest. Cash settled.

LIQUIDITY	**LEVERAGE**	**VOLATILITY**
Medium	Low	High

EQUITY INDICES

FTSE MIB
Italy

FTSE MIB is the benchmark index for the Italian stock market. It measures the performance of 40 most liquid and capitalized stocks in the Italian market and captures approximately 80% of the country's market capitalization.

FUTURES

Symbol	FTMIB
Electronic Venue	MIFE
Exchange Name	Borsa Italiana (IDEM)
Contract Size	EUR 5.00 x Index
Tick Size	5
Tick Value	EUR 25
Quoted in	Index points

OPTIONS

Contract Size	EUR 2.5 x Index
Tick Size	1, 2 or 5 depending on Premium
Tick Value	EUR 2.5, 5 or 25

Day Session | Monday to Friday: 9:00 a.m. to 5:50 p.m. Central European Time - Rome

TRADING TIPS

Individual constituents come from the Oil & Gas, Electricity, Banks, Insurance, Telecoms, Industrial Metals & Mining, and Personal Goods sectors among others. Cash settled.

LIQUIDITY   LEVERAGE   VOLATILITY

Low   Low   High

Equity Indices

CAC40 Index
France

CAC 40 comprises 40 constituents from the top 100 most active and capitalized stocks listed on Euronext Paris. This is the main benchmark of economic performance in France. Sectors: Pharmaceuticals, Oil & Gas, Banks, and Clothing among others.

FUTURES

Symbol	FCE
Electronic Venue	EURONEXT
Exchange Name	EURONEXT- Paris
Contract Size	EUR 10.00 x Index
Tick Size	0.5
Tick Value	EUR 5
Quoted in	Index points

Day Session | Monday to Friday: 8:00 a.m. to 10:00 p.m. Central European Time – Paris

OPTIONS

Contract Size	EUR 10.00 x Index
Tick Size	0.1
Tick Value	EUR 1

Day Session | Monday to Friday: 9:00 a.m. to 5:30 a.m. Central European Time - Paris

TRADING TIPS

A well-diversified index consisting of a surprisingly large number of international companies. Reacts positively to a low EUR/USD rate. Cash settled.

LIQUIDITY	**LEVERAGE**	**VOLATILITY**
High	Medium	High

EQUITY INDICES

SPI 200

Australia

The S&P/ASX 200 Index provides a broad benchmark while retaining the liquidity characteristics of narrower indexes. Quarterly updates effective from the third Friday of December.

FUTURES

Symbol	AP
Electronic Venue	ASX
Exchange Name	ASX Trade24
Contract Size	AUD 25.00 x Index
Tick Size	1
Tick Value	AUD 25
Quoted in	Index points

OPTIONS

Contract Size	One futures contract
Tick Size	0.5
Tick Value	AUD 12.5

Day Session | Monday to Friday: 9:30 a.m. – 4:30 p.m.
Night Session | Monday to Friday: 5:10 p.m. – 7:00 a.m*.
*extends to 8:00 a.m. from first Sunday in November to second Sunday in March | Eastern Daylight Time - Sydney

TRADING TIPS

The futures contract can hedge approximately 80% of the Australian equity market capitalization. Dividends of heavyweights can have an impact on pricing, so take extra care when calculating fair value. Cash settled.

LIQUIDITY	**LEVERAGE**	**VOLATILITY**
Medium	Medium	Medium

EQUITY INDICES

Bovespa
Brazil

Bovespa Index represents about 70% of Brazil's entire capitalization and is considered one of the biggest in the world. This is one of the leading indicators of Latin America's economic performance.

FUTURES

Symbol	IND
Electronic Venue	BMF
Exchange Name	Bolsa de Mercadorias e Futuros
Contract Size	BRL 1.00 x Index
Tick Size	5
Tick Value	BRL 5
Quoted in	Index points

OPTIONS

Contract Size	One futures contract
Tick Size	1
Tick Value	BRL 1

Day Session | Monday to Friday: 9:00 a.m. 5:55 p.m.
Brasilia Summer Time – Sao Paulo

TRADING TIPS

Commodities and exports are the main factors that move the Brazilian market. Attention should be given to inflation numbers and job reports. Cash settled.

LIQUIDITY   LEVERAGE   VOLATILITY

    High   Low   High

Equity Indices

CSI 300
China

The CSI300 index comprises the top 300 Chinese companies with the most liquid A shares on the Shanghai or Shenzhen stock exchanges. It was introduced in 2010 and was until recently the most heavily traded index future in the world. It is capitalization weighted.

FUTURES

Symbol	IF
Electronic Venue	CFFEX
Exchange Name	China Financial Futures Exch.
Contract Size	CNY 300.00 x Index
Tick Size	0.2
Tick Value	CNY 60
Quoted in	Index points

Day Session | Monday to Friday: 9:15 a.m. to 3:00 p.m. with a 1 ½ hour break from 11:30 a.m. to 1:00 p.m.
China Standard Time - Shanghai

TRADING TIPS

Comprised exclusively from large cap stocks and state-owned industrial conglomerates, the CSI 300 used to attract huge trading volume from all kinds of investors. Volumes dropped dramatically in the second half of 2015 following a short-selling ban.

LIQUIDITY   LEVERAGE   VOLATILITY

Medium   Low   High

EQUITY INDICES

Hang Seng
Hong Kong

Launched in 1969, the Hang Seng is a measure of overall performance of the Hong Kong stock market. The index is weighted by market capitalization.

FUTURES

Symbol	HSI
Electronic Venue	HKFE
Exchange Name	Hong Kong Futures Exchange
Contract Size	HKD 50.00 x Index
Tick Size	1
Tick Value	HKD 50
Quoted in	Index points

OPTIONS

Contract Size	HKD 50.00 x Index
Tick Size	1
Tick Value	HKD 50

Day Session | Monday to Friday: 9:15 a.m. to 4:15 p.m. with a one hour break from 12:00 p.m. to 1:00 p.m.
Hong Kong Time – Hong Kong

TRADING TIPS

The broad gauge of the Hong Kong stock market. The Hang Seng index is widely followed by overseas institutional investors, who account for about half of the volume. Cash settled.

LIQUIDITY	**LEVERAGE**	**VOLATILITY**
High	Low	High

EQUITY INDICES

H-shares
Hong Kong

H-Shares Index tracks the performance of mainland China enterprises traded on the Hong Kong Stock Exchange.

FUTURES

Symbol	HHI
Electronic Venue	HKFE
Exchange Name	Hong Kong Futures Exchange
Contract Size	HKD 50.00 x Index
Tick Size	1
Tick Value	HKD 50
Quoted in	Index points

OPTIONS

Contract Size	HKD 50.00 x Index
Tick Size	1
Tick Value	HKD 50

Day Session | Monday to Friday: 9:15 a.m. to 4:15 p.m. with a one hour break from 12:00 p.m. to 1:00 p.m.
Hong Kong Time – Hong Kong

TRADING TIPS

A convenient way for non-Chinese investors to trade the Chinese market. Watch out for arbitrage moves between the H-shares listed in Hong Kong and the A-shares listed in China. Cash settled.

LIQUIDITY	**LEVERAGE**	**VOLATILITY**
High	Low	High

Equity Indices

KOSPI 200
South Korea

The KOSPI 200 is the most liquid index in South Korea and among the most liquid index futures in the world. Regulatory changes in the options market in 2011 dumped retail activity and resulted in a dramatic drop of trading volumes. Korea has strong shipbuilding, automobile, mining and construction sectors.

FUTURES

Symbol	101
Electronic Venue	KRX
Exchange Name	Korea Exchange
Contract Size	KRW 500,000.00 x Index
Tick Size	0.05
Tick Value	KRW 25000
Quoted in	Index points

OPTIONS

Contract Size	KRW 500,000.00 x Index
Tick Size	0.05 for 3 or more points
Tick Value	KRW 25000

Day Session | Monday to Friday: 9:00 a.m. – 3:15 p.m.
Korea Standard Time – Seoul

TRADING TIPS

A weak Japanese yen can have a negative impact on Korea's competitiveness on exports. Cash settled.

LIQUIDITY   LEVERAGE   VOLATILITY
High   Low   Medium

EQUITY INDICES

Malaysia KLCI
Malaysia

The FTSE Bursa Malaysia KLCI is the benchmark of the Malaysian market, made from 30 of the largest Malaysian companies. The free floating market capitalization represents about 60% of the main market.

FUTURES

Symbol	FKLI
Electronic Venue	BMD
Exchange Name	Bursa Malaysia
Contract Size	MYR 50.00 x Index
Tick Size	0.5
Tick Value	MYR 25
Quoted in	Index points

OPTIONS

Contract Size	MYR 50.00 x Index
Tick Size	0.1
Tick Value	MYR 5

Day Session | Monday to Friday: 8:45 a.m. to 5:15 p.m. with a 1 hour 45 min break from 12:45 p.m. to 2:30 p.m. Malaysia Time – Kuala Lumpur

TRADING TIPS

A well-diversified index with Banking, Industrials, Telecoms, Electricity, Hotels, Farming & Fishing and Chemicals sectors among others. Cash settled.

LIQUIDITY	**LEVERAGE**	**VOLATILITY**
Medium	Medium	Low

EQUITY INDICES

CNX Nifty
India

S&P CNX Nifty: the Nifty 50 benchmarks of Indian equity. The largest index in India provides the underlying for offshore and onshore exchange traded funds, futures and options, other index funds, and over the counter (OTC) derivatives. Since 2009 computations have been based on free float market capitalization.

FUTURES

Symbol	NIFTY
Electronic Venue	NSE
Exchange Name	National Stock Exchange of India
Contract Size	INR 50.00 x Index
Tick Size	0.05
Tick Value	INR 2.5
Quoted in	

OPTIONS

Contract Size	INR 50.00 x Index
Tick Size	0.05
Tick Value	INR 2.5

Day Session | Monday to Friday: 9:15 a.m. to 3:30 p.m. India Standard Time – Mumbai

TRADING TIPS

An active futures market but with relatively high fluctuations in volume compared to markets of similar size and popularity. Suitable for retail and institutional investors alike. Cash settled.

LIQUIDITY	**LEVERAGE**	**VOLATILITY**
High	Low	High

EQUITY INDICES

AEX Index
Netherlands

A main index on NYSE Euronext and the most widely used indicator of Dutch Stock performance. It comprises the 25 most active securities in the Netherlands.

FUTURES

Symbol	FTI
Electronic Venue	EURONEXT
Exchange Name	EURONEXT - Amsterdam
Contract Size	EUR 200.00 x Index
Tick Size	0.05
Tick Value	EUR 10
Quoted in	Index points

OPTIONS

Contract Size	EUR 100.00 x Index
Tick Size	0.05
Tick Value	EUR 5

Day Session | Monday to Friday: 8:00 a.m. – 10:00 p.m. Central European Time - Amsterdam

TRADING TIPS

Oil and gas, food products and life insurance comprise more than 30% of the market capitalization. Cash settled.

LIQUIDITY	**LEVERAGE**	**VOLATILITY**
Medium	Medium	High

EQUITY INDICES

OMXS30
Sweden

Sweden's largest capitalized shares are here. Revised twice a year. Market weighted, so moves come from the larger companies.

FUTURES

Symbol	OMXS30
Electronic Venue	OMX
Exchange Name	OMX Nordic Exchange
Contract Size	Stockholm
Tick Size	SEK 100.00 x Index
Tick Value	0.25
Quoted in	SEK 25

OPTIONS

Contract Size	SEK 100.00 x Index
Tick Size	0.01
Tick Value	SEK 1

Day Session | Monday to Friday: 9:00 a.m. – 5:25 p.m. Central European Time - Stockholm

TRADING TIPS

Low national debt, stable inflation and a healthy banking system are important attributes of the Swedish economy. However, a soaring Swedish Krona puts pressure on exporters. Cash settled.

LIQUIDITY   LEVERAGE   VOLATILITY
Medium   Medium   High

EQUITY INDICES

Nikkei 225 Mini
Japan

The Nikkei 225 Mini (trading in Japan) was initiated in 1950. A price weighted index and the most widely recognized index in Japan. Calculated from a selection of 225 domestic common stocks listed on Tokyo Stock Exchange, reviewed annually and reshuffled usually in October.

FUTURES

Symbol	NK225M
Electronic Venue	OSE
Exchange Name	Osaka Securities Exchange
Contract Size	JPY 100.00 x Index
Tick Size	5
Tick Value	JPY 500
Quoted in	Index points

Day Session | Monday to Friday: 9:00 a.m. – 3:10 p.m.
Night Session | Monday to Friday: 4:30 p.m. to 2:55 a.m. next day.
Japan Standard Time – Tokyo

TRADING TIPS

Nikkei 225 mini is the most liquid futures market in Asia. Denominated in Yen. This futures market is one of the favorites of Japanese traders. Cash settled.

LIQUIDITY	**LEVERAGE**	**VOLATILITY**
High	High	Medium

EQUITY INDICES

RTS Index
Russia

The composite of the Russian stock market. Launched in 1995 it is reported by dollars in real-time on Moscow Interbank Currency Exchange. Trade the future to speculate the move of the 50 most liquid and capitalized Russian stocks.

FUTURES

Symbol	RIH2
Electronic Venue	RTS
Exchange Name	Moscow Exchange
Contract Size	USD 0.02 x Index
Tick Size	10
Tick Value	USD 0.20
Quoted in	Index points

OPTIONS

Contract Size	One futures contract
Tick Size	10
Tick Value	USD 0.20

Day Session | Monday to Friday: 10:00 a.m. – 6:45 p.m.
Night Session | Monday to Friday: 7:00 p.m. – 11:50 p.m.
Moscow Standard Time - Moscow

TRADING TIPS

A heavily traded market with energy stocks and financials weighing more than 60% of the market capitalization. A highly volatile stock market denominated in a highly volatile currency. Cash settled.

LIQUIDITY   LEVERAGE   VOLATILITY
High   Medium   High

Equity Indices

TAIEX
Taiwan

The TAIEX index is a capitalization-weighted index of all listed common shares traded on the Taiwan Stock Exchange. The most widely quoted of all TWSE indices.

FUTURES

Symbol	TXF
Electronic Venue	TAIFEX
Exchange Name	Taiwan Futures Exchange
Contract Size	TWD 200.00 x Index
Tick Size	1
Tick Value	TWD 200
Quoted in	Index points

OPTIONS

Contract Size	TWD 50.00 x Index
Tick Size	0.1
Tick Value	TWD 5

Day Session | Monday to Friday: 8:45 a.m. – 1:45 p.m. China Standard Time - Taipei

TRADING TIPS

The benchmark index of the Taiwanese market. High volume and accessible to foreign institutions. As with most Asian economies, Taiwan relies heavily on exports to China. Cash settled.

LIQUIDITY   LEVERAGE   VOLATILITY

High   Medium   Medium

EQUITY INDICES

WIG20
Poland

The WIG20 Index comprises the 20 major and most liquid companies in the Warsaw Stock Exchange Main List. It is a price index with main components coming from the Finance, Mining, Insurance and Telecoms sectors among others.

FUTURES

Symbol	WIG20
Electronic Venue	WSE
Exchange Name	Warsaw Stock Exchange
Contract Size	PLN 20.00 x Index
Tick Size	1
Tick Value	PLN 20
Quoted in	Index points

OPTIONS

Contract Size	PLN 20.00 x Index
Tick Size	1
Tick Value	PLN 20

Day Session | Monday to Friday: 8:45 a.m. – 5:05 p.m.
Central European Time - Warsaw

TRADING TIPS

A relatively stable market. Lacks depth and significant foreign participation. Recently certified by the CFTC, so US investor participation may increase. Cash settled.

LIQUIDITY	**LEVERAGE**	**VOLATILITY**
Low	Medium	Medium

EQUITY INDICES

FTSE Athens
Greece

The FTSE/ATHEX was previously known as the FTSE 20. After a number of mergers and delistings in the financial sector the issuer expanded its listings. It is now composed of 25 of the largest capitalization stocks in the Athens stock exchange.

FUTURES

Symbol	FTASE
Electronic Venue	ATHEX
Exchange Name	Athens Derivative Exchange
Contract Size	EUR 2.00 x Index
Tick Size	0.25
Tick Value	EUR 0.5
Quoted in	Index points

OPTIONS

Contract Size	EUR 2.00 x Index
Tick Size	0.25
Tick Value	EUR 0.5

Day Session | Monday to Friday: 10:10 a.m. – 5:20 p.m. Eastern European Time - Athens

TRADING TIPS

High volatility and low liquidity discourages participation from institutional investors. The recent rebase of the index value is a step in the right direction. Cash settled.

LIQUIDITY	LEVERAGE	VOLATILITY
Low	Low	High

EQUITY INDICES

S&P TSX 60
Canada

The S&P/TSX 60 Index contains the 60 largest companies listed on the Toronto Stock Exchange. This benchmark covers two-thirds of the total capitalization.

FUTURES

Symbol	SXF
Electronic Venue	MFE
Exchange Name	Montréal Exchange
Contract Size	CAD 200 x Index
Tick Size	0.1
Tick Value	CAD 20
Quoted in	Index points

Day Session | Monday to Friday: 6:00 a.m. – 4:15 p.m. with a 15 min break from 9:15 a.m. to 9:30 a.m.
Eastern Standard Time – Montreal

OPTIONS

Contract Size	CAD 10 x Index point
Tick Size	0.01
Tick Value	CAD 0.10

Day Session | Monday to Friday: 9:31 a.m. – 4:15 p.m.
Eastern Standard Time - Montreal

TRADING TIPS
Includes companies from the financials, energy, industrials and materials sectors among others. Cash settled.

LIQUIDITY   LEVERAGE   VOLATILITY
Medium   High   Low

Category 7 - Volatility

VOLATILITY

CBOE Volatility (VIX)
United States of America

VIX Index: A pure play on implied volatility independent of the direction and level of stock prices. Based on real-time prices of options on the S&P 500 Index, and designed to reflect investors' view of future volatility.

FUTURES

Symbol	VX
Electronic Venue	CBOE Command
Exchange Name	CBOE Futures Exchange
Contract Size	USD 1,000
Tick Size	0.05
Tick Value	USD 50
Quoted in	points

Continuous | Sunday to Friday: 5:00 p.m. - 3:15 p.m. with a 15 min break at 3:15 p.m. every day except Friday
Central Standard Time - Chicago

OPTIONS

Contract Size	100
Tick Size	0.05
Tick Value	USD 5

Day Session | Monday to Friday: 8:30 a.m. – 3:15 p.m.
Night Session | Monday to Friday: 2:00 a.m. to 8:15 a.m.
Central Standard Time - Chicago

TRADING TIPS

Widely known as "The Fear Index". The key point to remember is that it reflects consensus view of future, expected stock market volatility. Cash settled.

LIQUIDITY	**LEVERAGE**	**VOLATILITY**
High	Low	High

Category 8 - Interest Rates

INTEREST RATES

30-Day Fed Funds
United States of America

Federal funds or Fed Funds are overnight borrowings by banks to maintain their reserves at the Federal Reserve. Fed Funds futures are used speculatively to anticipate changes in short-term interest rates brought by changes in the Federal Reserve's monetary policy.

FUTURES

Symbol	ZQ
Electronic Venue	CME-CBT
Exchange Name	Chicago Board of Trade
Contract Size	USD 5,000,000.00
Tick Size	One quarter of one basis point
Tick Value	USD 10.4175
Quoted in	100 - yield

OPTIONS

Contract Size	One futures contract
Tick Size	0.0025
Tick Value	USD 10.4175

Continuous | Sunday to Friday: 5:00 p.m. – 4:00 p.m. with a 1 hour break from 4:00 p.m. to 5:00 p.m. every day except Friday, which closes at 4:00 p.m.
Central Standard Time - Chicago

TRADING TIPS

Quoted as 100 – yield, the Fed Fund futures are highly liquid and suitable for professional investors. Cash settled.

LIQUIDITY	**LEVERAGE**	**VOLATILITY**
High	High	Low

INTEREST RATES
Eurodollar
United States of America

Three-month time deposits in USD at banks outside the United States.

FUTURES

Symbol	GE
Electronic Venue	GLOBEX
Exchange Name	Chicago Mercantile Exchange
Contract Size	USD 1,000,000.00
Tick Size	0.005
Tick Value	USD 12.5
Quoted in	100 - yield

OPTIONS

Contract Size	One futures contract
Tick Size	0.0025
Tick Value	USD 6.25

Continuous | Sunday to Friday: 5:00 p.m. – 4:00 p.m. with a 1 hour break from 4:00 p.m. to 5:00 p.m. every day except Friday, which closes at 4:00 p.m.
Central Standard Time - Chicago

TRADING TIPS

Not to be confused with the EUR/USD exchange rate. Small moves and tight bid/ask spreads. Cash settled.

LIQUIDITY	**LEVERAGE**	**VOLATILITY**
High	High	Low

INTEREST RATES

Three Month Euro (EURIBOR)
Great Britain

Euribor provides the daily average of Eurozone banks' lending rates to banks. The benchmark rate for mortgages, interest rate swaps and futures, and saving accounts.

FUTURES

Symbol	I
Electronic Venue	ICE
Exchange Name	ICE Futures - Europe
Contract Size	EUR 1,000,000.00
Tick Size	0.005
Tick Value	EUR 12.5
Quoted in	100 - yield

OPTIONS

Contract Size	One futures contract
Tick Size	0.005
Tick Value	EUR 12.5

Day Session | Monday to Friday: 1:00 a.m. – 9 p.m.
Greenwich Mean Time – London

TRADING TIPS
Euribor is distinct from Euro Libor. Small moves and tight bid/ask spreads make it hard to day-trade. Cash settled.

LIQUIDITY	**LEVERAGE**	**VOLATILITY**
High	High	Low

INTEREST RATES

Three Month Euro Swiss Franc-Euroswiss
Great Britain

Euroswiss is the LIBOR rate in Swiss francs with a maturity of 3 months. It is a valuable benchmark for determining interest rate differentials to help estimate exchange rates.

FUTURES

Symbol	S
Electronic Venue	ICE
Exchange Name	ICE Futures - Europe
Contract Size	CHF 1.000.000
Tick Size	0.01
Tick Value	CHF 25
Quoted in	100 - yield

OPTIONS

Contract Size	One futures contract
Tick Size	0.005
Tick Value	CHF 12.5

Day Session | Monday to Friday: 7:30 a.m. – 6:00 p.m. Greenwich Mean Time – London

TRADING TIPS

A professional's tool to hedge against interest rates in Swiss francs. Not to be confused with the Euro/Swiss exchange rate. Cash settled.

LIQUIDITY   LEVERAGE   VOLATILITY
High   High   Low

INTEREST RATES

Three Month Sterling (Short Sterling)
Great Britain

Short Sterling is the interest rate at which selected banks lend one another. The contract is priced at 100 minus the expected sterling rate for a maturity in 3 months.

FUTURES

Symbol	L
Electronic Venue	ICE
Exchange Name	ICE Futures -Europe
Contract Size	GBP 500,000.00
Tick Size	0.01
Tick Value	GBP 12.5
Quoted in	100 - yield

OPTIONS

Contract Size	One futures contract
Tick Size	0.005
Tick Value	GBP 6.25

Day Session | Monday to Friday: 7:30 a.m. − 6:00 p.m. Greenwich Mean Time − London

TRADING TIPS

"Short" stands for short term. A rate of 1% will be quoted at 99 (100-1). Cash settled.

LIQUIDITY   LEVERAGE   VOLATILITY
High   High   Low

Category 9 - Livestock

LIVESTOCK
Live Cattle
United States of America

A multi-billion dollar industry. Cattle are used to produce beef, milk, cheese, yoghurt and other dairy produce. They have been fed high energy rations to meet US consumer preferences. In1964, the Chicago Mercantile Exchange (CME) introduced the first futures contract.

FUTURES

Symbol	LE
Electronic Venue	GLOBEX
Exchange Name	Chicago Mercantile Exchange
Contract Size	40,000.00 lbs
Tick Size	0.00025
Tick Value	USD 10
Quoted in	USD/lb.

OPTIONS

Contract Size	One futures contract
Tick Size	0.00025
Tick Value	USD 10

Day Session | Monday to Friday: 8:30 a.m. – 1:05 p.m. Central Standard Time - Chicago

TRADING TIPS
The top 7 cattle and beef producers are the US, Brazil, EU, China, Argentina, India, and Australia. An ideal hedging instrument for cattle producers and those in the food industry. Physical delivery.

LIQUIDITY   **LEVERAGE**   **VOLATILITY**
Medium   High   Medium

LIVESTOCK

Lean Hog

United States of America

Refers to industrially raised hogs (pigs). The US is the world's largest pork exporter. Most hog production occurs in Iowa, North Carolina, Minnesota, and Illinois.

FUTURES

Symbol	HE
Electronic Venue	GLOBEX
Exchange Name	Chicago Mercantile Exchange
Contract Size	40,000.00 lbs
Tick Size	0.00025
Tick Value	USD 10
Quoted in	USD/lb.

OPTIONS

Contract Size	One futures contract
Tick Size	0.00025
Tick Value	USD 10

Day Session | Monday to Friday: 8:30 a.m. – 1:05 p.m. Central Standard Time - Chicago

TRADING TIPS

An ideal hedging instrument for hog producers. USDA reports and consumer food trends are important determinants of prices. Cash settled.

LIQUIDITY	**LEVERAGE**	**VOLATILITY**
Low	Medium	High

Category 10 - Metals

METALS

Gold 100 oz.

United States of America

Gold is the most important monetary standard in the world. Held as an investment during monetary and political crises. Used in electronics and medicine. South Africa, US, Australia, Russia and Peru among the top producers.

FUTURES

Symbol	GC
Electronic Venue	GLOBEX
Exchange Name	Commodity Exchange, Inc.
Contract Size	100.00 troy ounces
Tick Size	0.1
Tick Value	USD 10
Quoted in	USD/troy ounce

OPTIONS

Contract Size	One futures contract
Tick Size	0.1
Tick Value	USD 10

Continuous | Sunday to Friday: 6:00 p.m. to 5:00 p.m. with a 60 min break from 5:00 p.m. to 6:00 p.m. every day except Friday, which closes at 5:00 p.m.
Eastern Standard Time - New York

TRADING TIPS

A vibrant futures market with participants from every corner of the world. Inventories, the US Dollar, mining, inflation expectations all play an equally important role in price discovery. Physical delivery.

LIQUIDITY	**LEVERAGE**	**VOLATILITY**
High	High	Medium

Metals

Copper
United States of America

Copper is an important economic indicator due to its use in construction and industrial machinery manufacturing. It is widely used in electronics, plumbing and heating. Asia is the world's largest producing region.

FUTURES

Symbol	HG
Electronic Venue	GLOBEX
Exchange Name	Commodity Exchange, Inc.
Contract Size	25,000.00 lbs
Tick Size	0.05
Tick Value	USD 12.5
Quoted in	USD/lb.

OPTIONS

Contract Size	One futures contract
Tick Size	0.05
Tick Value	USD 12.5

Continuous | Sunday to Friday: 6:00 p.m. to 5:00 p.m. with a 60 min break from 5:00 p.m. to 6:00 p.m. every day except Friday, which closes at 5:00 p.m.
Eastern Standard Time - New York

TRADING TIPS

CFTC reports offer a great deal of information on copper's long and short positions in COMEX sorted by trader category. One should also monitor other exchanges of active copper trading, such as that of Shanghai's. Physical delivery.

LIQUIDITY	LEVERAGE	VOLATILITY
Medium	Medium	High

METALS

Silver

United States of America

Silver is widely held in diversified and smart investment portfolios. Used extensively in the photographic, jewelry, and electronic industries with Mexico, Peru, and China the major producers.

FUTURES

Symbol	SI
Electronic Venue	GLOBEX
Exchange Name	Commodity Exchange, Inc.
Contract Size	5,000.00 troy ounces
Tick Size	0.005
Tick Value	USD 25
Quoted in	USD/troy ounce

OPTIONS

Contract Size	One futures contact
Tick Size	0.001
Tick Value	USD 5

Continuous | Sunday to Friday: 6:00 p.m. to 5:00 p.m. with a 60 min break from 5:00 p.m. to 6:00 p.m. every day except Friday, which closes at 5:00 p.m.
Eastern Standard Time - New York

TRADING TIPS

Highly correlated with the price of gold but one can never be sure in the short term. Nevertheless, gold to silver ratio is used widely for comparison purposes. Physical delivery.

LIQUIDITY	**LEVERAGE**	**VOLATILITY**
Medium	Low	High

METALS
Mini Gold
United States of America

(Mini) Gold is the most important monetary standard in the world. Held as an investment during monetary and political crises. Used in electronics and medicine. South Africa, US, Australia, Russia and Peru among the top producers.

FUTURES

Symbol	CFYG
Electronic Venue	ICE
Exchange Name	ICE Futures U.S.
Contract Size	33.20 troy ounces
Tick Size	0.1
Tick Value	USD 3.328
Quoted in	USD/troy ounce

Continuous |Sunday to Friday: 6:00 p.m. − 6:00 p.m. with a 2-hour break from 6:00 p.m. to 8:00 p.m. every weekday except Friday, which closes at 6:00 p.m.
Eastern Standard Time - New York

TRADING TIPS

An attractive alternative to the large gold contract, yet low volume requires extra attention. Physical delivery.

LIQUIDITY	**LEVERAGE**	**VOLATILITY**
Low	High	Medium

METALS

Mini Silver

United States of America

(Mini) Silver is widely held in diversified and alternative investment portfolios. Used extensively in the photographic, jewelry, and electronic industries with Mexico, Peru, and China the major producers.

FUTURES

Symbol	CFYI
Electronic Venue	ICE
Exchange Name	ICE Futures U.S.
Contract Size	1,000.00 troy ounces
Tick Size	0.001
Tick Value	USD 1
Quoted in	USD/troy ounce

Continuous | Sunday to Friday: 6:00 p.m. – 6:00 p.m. with a 2-hour break from 6:00 p.m. to 8:00 p.m. every weekday except Friday, which closes at 6:00 p.m.
Eastern Standard Time - New York

TRADING TIPS

One-fifth of the size of the COMEX Silver contract. Like the mini gold contract, the mini silver is weak on volumes. Physical delivery.

LIQUIDITY   LEVERAGE   VOLATILITY

Low   Low   High

METALS

Palladium
United States of America

Palladium is part of the platinum metal group. Russia, South Africa, Canada and the US are major producers. It is used in catalytic converters.

FUTURES

Symbol	PA
Electronic Venue	GLOBEX
Exchange Name	New York Mercantile Exchange
Contract Size	100.00 troy ounces
Tick Size	0.05
Tick Value	USD 5
Quoted in	

OPTIONS

Contract Size	One futures contract
Tick Size	0.05
Tick Value	USD 5

Continuous | Sunday to Friday: 6:00 p.m. to 5:00 p.m. with a 60 min break from 5:00 p.m. to 6:00 p.m. every day except Friday, which closes at 5:00 p.m.
Eastern Standard Time - New York

TRADING TIPS

Palladium is a very volatile commodity. More than 80% of production is concentrated in Russia and South Africa. Growing car sales tend to drive Palladium prices higher. Physical delivery.

LIQUIDITY   LEVERAGE   VOLATILITY
Low   Low   High

Category 11 – Softs

SOFTS

Sugar No. 11

United States of America

Sugar No. 11 refers to world sugar prices, which can be heavily influenced by governments. Sugar's role in ethanol production makes it both an energy commodity and a food commodity.

FUTURES

Symbol	SB
Electronic Venue	ICE
Exchange Name	ICE Futures US Softs
Contract Size	112,000.00 lbs
Tick Size	0.01
Tick Value	USD 11.2
Quoted in	USD/lb.

OPTIONS

Contract Size	One futures contract
Tick Size	0.01
Tick Value	USD 11.2

Day Session | Monday to Friday: 3:30 a.m. – 1:00 p.m. Eastern Standard Time – New York

TRADING TIPS

The lag between supply and demand decisions, known as the cobweb theorem relates to most commodities including sugar. The hedging instrument of choice by major soft-drink producers. Physical delivery.

LIQUIDITY	LEVERAGE	VOLATILITY
Medium	Low	High

SOFTS

Cocoa
United States of America

Cocoa is a critical export for the economies of many West African countries. Processing is done mainly in the Ivory Coast, Netherlands and the US. However, a recent trend to increase processing at origin countries is expected to reduce costs of exporters.

FUTURES

Symbol	CC
Electronic Venue	ICE
Exchange Name	ICE Futures US Softs
Contract Size	10.00 Metric Tons
Tick Size	1
Tick Value	USD 10
Quoted in	USD/metric ton

OPTIONS

Contract Size	One futures contract
Tick Size	1
Tick Value	USD 10

Day Session | Monday to Friday: 4:45 a.m. – 1:30 p.m. Eastern Standard Time - New York

TRADING TIPS

The amount and distribution of rainfall is the most important factor in determining the yield of cocoa trees from year to year. Cocoa is correlated more to the GBP than to the US Dollar index. Physical delivery.

LIQUIDITY	LEVERAGE	VOLATILITY
Medium	Medium	High

SOFTS

Coffee C
United States of America

Coffee is the second most commonly traded commodity after crude oil. The "C" contract is the world's benchmark for the Arabica variety. Major coffee producers include Brazil, Central America, Caribbean, Colombia and sub-Sahara countries.

FUTURES

Symbol	KC
Electronic Venue	ICE
Exchange Name	ICE Futures US Softs
Contract Size	37,500.00 lbs
Tick Size	0.05
Tick Value	USD 18.75
Quoted in	USD/lb.

OPTIONS

Contract Size	One futures contract
Tick Size	0.01
Tick Value	USD 3.75

Day Session | Monday to Friday: 4:15 a.m. – 1:30 p.m. Eastern Standard Time - New York

TRADING TIPS

Weather conditions in Brazil and Colombia should be monitored carefully. An old saying goes "never be short coffee going into July". Physical delivery.

LIQUIDITY	**LEVERAGE**	**VOLATILITY**
Low	Low	High

SOFTS

Cotton No. 2
United States of America

Cotton No 2 is considered the benchmark for trading this important global commodity. US subsidies, China's insatiable demand and water shortages play a significant role in cotton's advancement.

FUTURES

Symbol	CT
Electronic Venue	ICE
Exchange Name	ICE Futures US Softs
Contract Size	50,000.00 lbs
Tick Size	0.01
Tick Value	USD 5
Quoted in	USD/lb.

OPTIONS

Contract Size	One futures contract
Tick Size	0.01
Tick Value	USD 5

Continuous | Sunday to Friday: 9:00 p.m. – 2:20 p.m. with a 6 hour and 40 min break from 2:20 p.m. to 9:00 p.m. every day except Friday, which closes at 2:20 p.m.
Eastern Standard Time – New York

TRADING TIPS

Supply and demand expectations move all markets. Cotton is no exception. USDA reports, inventories, government policies and price of subsidies should be monitored closely. Physical delivery.

LIQUIDITY	**LEVERAGE**	**VOLATILITY**
Medium	Medium	High

INDEX

10-Year T-Note	31
2-Year T-Note	33
30-Day Fed Funds	98
5-Year T-Note	32
AEX Index	86
AUD/USD	47
Bean Oil	21
BIST 30	67
Bovespa	79
Brent Crude	60
CAC40 Index	77
CAD/USD	54
CBOE Volatility (VIX)	96
CHF/USD	48
CNX Nifty	85

Cocoa	117
Coffee C	118
Copper	109
Corn	18
Cotton No. 2	119
CSI 300	80
DAX	64
E-mini Crude Oil	62
E-mini Dow ($5)	68
E-mini EUR/USD	49
E-mini JPY/USD	50
E-mini Natural Gas	61
Emissions	56
EUR/CHF	46
EUR/GBP	45
EUR/JPY	44
EUR/USD	41
Euro-Bobl	28

Euro-BTP	26
Euro-Bund	27
Eurodollar	99
Euro-Oat	39
Euro-Schatz	29
EuroStoxx 50	65
Five-Year Government of Canada Bond	36
FTSE 100	73
FTSE Athens	92
FTSE MIB	76
GBP/USD	42
Gold 100 oz	108
Hang Seng	81
Henry Hub Natural Gas	59
H-shares	82
IBEX	74
JPY/USD	43
KOSPI 200	83

Lean Hog	105
Light Sweet Crude Oil	58
Live Cattle	104
Long Gilt	37
Malaysia KLCI	84
Micro EUR/USD	53
Mini FTSE MIB	75
Mini Gold	111
Mini NASDAQ 100	70
Mini Russell 2000	71
Mini S&P 500	69
Mini Silver	112
MXN/USD	52
Nikkei 225	72
Nikkei 225 Mini	88
NZD/USD	51
Oat	23
OMXS30	87

Palladium	113
Rough Rice	24
RTS Index	89
S&P TSX 60	93
Short Gilt	38
Silver	110
SMI	66
Soybean	19
Soybean Meal	22
SPI 200	78
Sugar No. 11	116
TAIEX	90
Ten-Year Government of Canada Bond	34
Three Month Euro (EURIBOR)	100
Three Month Euro Swiss Franc-Euroswiss	101
Three Month Sterling (Short Sterling)	102
Two-Year Government of Canada Bond	35
U.S. Treasury Bond	30

Wheat	20
WIG20	91

NOTES

www.ingramcontent.com/pod-product-compliance
Lightning Source LLC
Chambersburg PA
CBHW070257190526
45169CB00001B/441